THE SMALL CATECHISM

By MARTIN LUTHER

The Small Catechism
By Martin Luther

Print ISBN 13: 978-1-4209-6904-7
eBook ISBN 13: 978-1-4209-6905-4

Cover Image: a detail of a portrait of Martin Luther, c. 16th century / G. Dagli Orti /De Agostini Picture Library / Bridgeman Images.

Please visit *www.digireads.com*

CONTENTS

Luther's Preface to the Small Catechism

Martin Luther to All Faithful and Godly Pastors and Preachers:

Grace, Mercy, and Peace in Jesus Christ, our Lord.

The deplorable, miserable condition which I discovered lately when I, too, was a visitor, has forced and urged me to prepare [publish] this Catechism, or Christian doctrine, in this small, plain, simple form. Mercy! Good God! what manifold misery I beheld! The common people, especially in the villages, have no knowledge whatever of Christian doctrine, and, alas! many pastors are altogether incapable and incompetent to teach [so much so, that one is ashamed to speak of it]. Nevertheless, all maintain that they are Christians, have been baptized and receive the [common] holy Sacraments. Yet they [*do not* understand and] cannot [*even*] recite either the Lord's Prayer, or the Creed, or the Ten Commandments; they live like dumb brutes and irrational hogs; and yet, now that the Gospel has come, they have nicely learned to abuse all liberty like experts.

O ye bishops! [to whom this charge has been committed by God,] what will ye ever answer to Christ for having so shamefully neglected the people and never for a moment discharged your office? [You are the persons to whom alone this ruin of the Christian religion is due. You have permitted men to err so shamefully; yours is the guilt; for you have ever done anything rather than what your office required you to do.] May all misfortune flee you! [I do not wish at this place to invoke evil on your heads.] You command the Sacrament in one form [but is not this the highest ungodliness coupled with the greatest impudence that you are insisting on the administration of the Sacrament in one form only, and on your traditions] and insist on your human laws, and yet at the same time you do not care in the least [while you are utterly without scruple and concern] whether the people know the Lord's Prayer, the Creed, the Ten Commandments, or any part of the Word of God. Woe, woe, unto you forever!

Therefore I entreat [and adjure] you all for God's sake, my dear sirs and brethren, who are pastors or preachers, to devote yourselves heartily to your office, to have pity on the people who are entrusted to you, and to help us inculcate the Catechism upon the people, and especially upon the young. And let those of you who cannot do better [If any of you are so unskilled that you have absolutely no knowledge of these matters, let them not be ashamed to] take these tables and forms and impress them, word for word, on the people, as follows:—

In the first place, let the preacher above all be careful to avoid many kinds of or various texts and forms of the Ten Commandments, the Lord's Prayer, the Creed, the Sacraments, etc., but choose one form to which he adheres, and which he inculcates all the time, year after year. For [I give this advice, however, because I know that] young and simple people must be taught by uniform, settled texts and forms, otherwise they easily become confused when the teacher to-day teaches them thus, and in a year some other way, as if he wished to make improvements, and thus all effort and labor [which has been expended in teaching] is lost.

Also our blessed fathers understood this well; for they all used the same form of the Lord's Prayer, the Creed, and the Ten Commandments. Therefore we, too, should [imitate their diligence and be at pains to] teach the young and simple people these parts in such a way as not to change a syllable, or set them forth and repeat them one year differently than in another [no matter how often we teach the Catechism].

Hence, choose whatever form you please, and adhere to it forever. But when you preach in the presence of learned and intelligent men, you may exhibit your skill, and may present these parts in as varied and intricate ways and give them as masterly turns as you are able. But with the young people stick to one fixed, permanent form and manner, and teach them, first of all, these parts, namely, the Ten Commandments, the Creed, the Lord's Prayer, etc., according to the text, word for word, so that they, too, can repeat it in the same manner after you and commit it to memory.

But those who are unwilling to learn it should be told that they deny Christ and are no Christians, neither should they be admitted to the Sacrament, accepted as sponsors at baptism, nor exercise any part of Christian liberty, but should simply be turned back to the Pope and his officials, yea, to the devil himself. Moreover, their parents and employers should refuse them food and drink, and [they would also do well if they were to] notify them that the prince will drive such rude people from the country, etc.

For although we cannot and should not force any one to believe, yet we should insist and urge the people that they know what is right and wrong with those among whom they dwell and wish to make their living. For whoever desires to reside in a town must know and observe the town laws, the protection of which he wishes to enjoy, no matter whether he is a believer or at heart and in private a rogue or knave.

In the second place, after they have well learned the text, then teach them the sense also, so that they know what it means, and again choose the form of these tables, or some other brief uniform method, whichever you like, and adhere to it, and do not change a single syllable, as was just said regarding the text; and take your time to it. For it is not necessary that you take up all the parts at once, but one after the other. After they understand the First Commandment well, then take up the Second, and so on, otherwise they will be overwhelmed, so as not to be able to retain any well.

In the third place, after you have thus taught them this Short Catechism, then take up the Large Catechism, and give them also a richer and fuller knowledge. Here explain at large every commandment, [article,] petition, and part with its various works, uses, benefits, dangers, and injuries, as you find these abundantly stated in many books written about these matters. And particularly, urge that commandment or part most which suffers the greatest neglect among your people. For instance, the Seventh Commandment, concerning stealing, must be strenuously urged among mechanics and merchants, and even farmers and servants, for among these people many kinds of dishonesty and thieving prevail. So, too, you must urge well the Fourth Commandment among the children and the common people, that they may be quiet and faithful, obedient and peaceable, and you must always adduce many examples from the Scriptures to show how God has punished or blessed such persons.

Especially should you here urge magistrates and parents to rule well and to send their children to school, showing them why it is their duty to do this, and what a damnable sin they are committing if they do not do it. For by such neglect they overthrow and destroy both the kingdom of God and that of the world, acting as the worst enemies both of God and of men. And make it very plain to them what an awful harm they are doing if they will not help to train children to be pastors, preachers, clerks [also for other offices, with which we cannot dispense in this life], etc., and that God will punish them terribly for it. For such preaching is needed. [Verily, I do not know of any other topic that deserves to be treated as much as this.] Parents and magistrates are now sinning unspeakably in this respect. The devil, too, aims at something cruel because of these things [that he may hurl Germany into the greatest distress].

Lastly, since the tyranny of the Pope has been abolished, people are no longer willing to go to the Sacrament and despise it [as something useless and unnecessary]. Here again urging is necessary, however, with this understanding: We are to force no one to believe, or to receive the Sacrament, nor fix any law, nor time, nor place for it, but are to preach in such a manner that of their own accord, without our law, they will urge themselves and, as it were, compel us pastors to administer the Sacrament. This is done by telling them: Whoever does not seek or desire the Sacrament at least some four times a year, it is to be feared that he despises the Sacrament and is no Christian, just as he is no Christian who does not believe or hear the Gospel; for Christ did not say, This omit, or, This despise, but, This do ye, as oft as ye drink it, etc. Verily, He wants it done, and not entirely neglected and despised. This do ye, He says.

Now, whoever does not highly value the Sacrament thereby shows that he has no sin, no flesh, no devil, no world, no death, no danger, no hell; that is, he does not believe any such things, although he is in them over head and ears and is doubly the devil's own. On the other hand, he needs no grace, life, Paradise, heaven, Christ, God, nor anything good. For if he believed that he had so much that is evil, and needed so much that is good, he would not thus neglect the Sacrament, by which such evil is remedied and so much good is bestowed. Neither will it be necessary to force him to the Sacrament by any law, but he will come running and racing of his own accord, will force himself and urge you that you must give him the Sacrament.

Hence, you must not make any law in this matter, as the Pope does. Only set forth clearly the benefit and harm, the need and use, the danger and the blessing, connected with this Sacrament, and the people will come of themselves without your compulsion. But if they do not come, let them go and tell them that such belong to the devil as do not regard nor feel their great need and the gracious help of God. But if you do not urge this, or make a law or a bane of it, it is your fault if they despise the Sacrament. How could they be otherwise than slothful if you sleep and are silent? Therefore look to it, ye pastors and preachers. Our office is now become a different thing from what it was under the Pope; it is now become serious and salutary. Accordingly, it now involves much more trouble and labor, danger and trials, and, in addition thereto, little reward and gratitude in the world. But Christ Himself will be our reward if we labor faithfully. To this end may the Father of all grace help us, to whom be praise and thanks forever through Christ, our Lord! Amen.

I. THE TEN COMMANDMENTS

As the head of the family should teach them in a simple way to his household.

The First Commandment.

Thou shalt have no other gods.

What does this mean?—Answer.

We should fear, love, and trust in God above all things.

The Second Commandment.

Thou shalt not take the name of the Lord, thy God, in vain.

What does this mean?—Answer.

We should fear and love God that we may not curse, swear, use witchcraft, lie, or deceive by His name, but call upon it in every trouble, pray, praise, and give thanks.

The Third Commandment.

Thou shalt sanctify the holy-day.

What does this mean?—Answer.

We should fear and love God that we may not despise preaching and His Word, but hold it sacred, and gladly hear and learn it.

The Fourth Commandment.

Thou shalt honor thy father and thy mother [that it may be well with thee and thou mayest live long upon the earth].

What does this mean?—Answer.

We should fear and love God that we may not despise nor anger our parents and masters, but give them honor, serve, obey, and hold them in love and esteem.

The Fifth Commandment.

Thou shalt not kill.

What does this mean?—Answer.

We should fear and love God that we may not hurt nor harm our neighbor in his body, but help and befriend him in every bodily need [in every need and danger of life and body].

The Sixth Commandment.

Thou shalt not commit adultery.

What does this mean?—Answer.

We should fear and love God that we may lead a chaste and decent life in words and deeds, and each love and honor his spouse.

The Seventh Commandment.

Thou shalt not steal.

What does this mean?—Answer.

We should fear and love God that we may not take our neighbor's money or property, nor get them by false ware or dealing, but help him to improve and protect his property and business [that his means are preserved and his condition is improved].

The Eighth Commandment.

Thou shalt not bear false witness against thy neighbor.

What does this mean?—Answer.

We should fear and love God that we may not deceitfully belie, betray, slander, or defame our neighbor, but defend him, [think and] speak well of him, and put the best construction on everything.

The Ninth Commandment.

Thou shalt not covet thy neighbor's house.

What does this mean?—Answer.

We should fear and love God that we may not craftily seek to get our neighbor's inheritance or house, and obtain it by a show of [justice and] right, etc., but help and be of service to him in keeping it.

The Tenth Commandment.

Thou shalt not covet thy neighbor's wife, nor his man-servant, nor his maid-servant, nor his cattle, nor anything that is his.

What does this mean?—Answer.

We should fear and love God that we may not estrange, force, or entice away our neighbor's wife, servants, or cattle, but urge them to stay and [diligently] do their duty.

What Does God Say of All These Commandments?

Answer.

He says thus (Exod. 20:5f): I the Lord, thy God, am a jealous God, visiting the iniquity of the fathers upon the children unto the third and fourth generation of them that hate Me, and showing mercy unto thousands of them that love Me and keep My commandments.

What does this mean?—Answer.

God threatens to punish all that transgress these commandments. Therefore we should dread His wrath and not act contrary to these commandments. But He promises grace and every blessing to all that keep these commandments. Therefore we should also love and trust in Him, and gladly do [zealously and diligently order our whole life] according to His commandments.

II. THE CREED

As the head of the family should teach it in a simple way to his household.

The First Article.

Of Creation.

I believe in God the Father Almighty, Maker of heaven and earth.

What does this mean?—Answer.

I believe that God has made me and all creatures; that He has given me my body and soul, eyes, ears, and all my limbs, my reason, and all my senses, and still preserves them; in addition thereto, clothing and shoes, meat and drink, house and homestead, wife and children, fields, cattle, and all my goods; that He provides me richly and daily with all that I need to support this body and life, protects me from all danger, and guards me and preserves me from all evil; and all this out of pure, fatherly, divine goodness and mercy, without any merit or worthiness in me; for all which I owe it to Him to thank, praise, serve, and obey Him. This is most certainly true.

The Second Article.

Of Redemption.

And in Jesus Christ, His only Son, our Lord; who was conceived by the Holy Ghost, born of the Virgin Mary; suffered under Pontius Pilate, was crucified, dead, and buried; He descended into hell; the third day He rose again from the dead; He ascended into heaven, and sitteth on the right hand of God the Father Almighty; from thence He shall come to judge the quick and the dead.

What does this mean?—Answer.

I believe that Jesus Christ, true God, begotten of the Father from eternity, and also true man, born of the Virgin Mary, is my Lord, who has redeemed me, a lost and condemned creature, purchased and won [delivered] me from all sins, from death, and from the power of the devil, not with gold or silver, but with His holy, precious blood and with His innocent suffering and death, in order that I may be [wholly] His own, and live under Him in His kingdom, and serve Him in everlasting righteousness, innocence, and blessedness, even as He is risen from the dead, lives and reigns to all eternity. This is most certainly true.

The Third Article.

Of Sanctification.

I believe in the Holy Ghost; one holy Christian Church, the communion of saints; the forgiveness of sins; the resurrection of the body; and the life everlasting. Amen.

What does this mean?—Answer.

I believe that I cannot by my own reason or strength believe in Jesus Christ, my Lord, or come to Him; but the Holy Ghost has called me by the Gospel, enlightened me with His gifts, sanctified and kept me in the true faith; even as He calls, gathers, enlightens, and sanctifies the whole Christian Church on earth, and keeps it with Jesus Christ in the one true faith; in which Christian Church He forgives daily and richly all sins to me and all believers, and at the last day will raise up me and all the dead, and will give to me and to all believers in Christ everlasting life. This is most certainly true.

III. THE LORD'S PRAYER

As the head of the family should teach it in a simple way to his household.

Our Father who art in heaven.

What does this mean?—Answer.

God would thereby [with this little introduction] tenderly urge us to believe that He is our true Father, and that we are His true children, so that we may ask Him confidently with all assurance, as dear children ask their dear father.

The First Petition.

Hallowed be Thy name.

What does this mean?—Answer.

God's name is indeed holy in itself; but we pray in this petition that it may become holy among us also.

How is this done?—Answer.

When the Word of God is taught in its truth and purity, and we as the children of God also lead holy lives in accordance with it. To this end help us, dear Father in heaven. But he that teaches and lives otherwise than God's Word teaches profanes the name of God among us. From this preserve us, Heavenly Father.

The Second Petition.

Thy kingdom come.

What does this mean?—Answer.

The kingdom of God comes indeed without our prayer, of itself; but we pray in this petition that it may come unto us also.

How is this done?—Answer.

When our heavenly Father gives us His Holy Spirit, so that by His grace we believe His holy Word and lead a godly life here in time and yonder in eternity.

The Third Petition.

Thy will be done on earth as it is in heaven.

What does this mean?—Answer.

The good and gracious will of God is done indeed without our prayer; but we pray in this petition that it may be done among us also.

How is this done?—Answer.

When God breaks and hinders every evil counsel and will which would not let us hallow the name of God nor let His kingdom come, such as the will of the devil, the world, and our flesh; but strengthens and keeps us steadfast in His Word and in faith unto our end. This is His gracious and good will.

The Fourth Petition.

Give us this day our daily bread.

What does this mean?—Answer.

God gives daily bread, even without our prayer, to all wicked men; but we pray in this petition that He would lead us to know it, and to receive our daily bread with thanksgiving.

What is meant by daily bread?—Answer.

Everything that belongs to the support and wants of the body, such as meat, drink, clothing, shoes, house, homestead, field, cattle, money, goods, a pious spouse, pious children, pious servants, pious and faithful magistrates, good government, good weather, peace, health, discipline, honor, good friends, faithful neighbors, and the like.

The Fifth Petition.

And forgive us our trespasses, as we forgive those who trespass against us.

What does this mean?—Answer.

We pray in this petition that our Father in heaven would not look upon our sins, nor deny such petitions on account of them; for we are worthy of none of the things for which we pray, neither have we deserved them; but that He would grant them all to us by grace; for we daily sin much, and indeed deserve nothing but punishment. So will we verily, on our part, also heartily forgive and also readily do good to those who sin against us.

The Sixth Petition.

And lead us not into temptation.

What does this mean?—Answer.

God, indeed, tempts no one; but we pray in this petition that God would guard and keep us, so that the devil, the world, and our flesh may not deceive us, nor seduce us into misbelief, despair, and other great shame and vice; and though we be assailed by them, that still we may finally overcome and gain the victory.

The Seventh Petition.

But deliver us from evil.

What does this mean?—Answer.

We pray in this petition, as in a summary, that our Father in heaven would deliver us from all manner of evil, of body and soul, property and honor, and at last, when our last hour shall come, grant us a blessed end, and graciously take us from this vale of tears to Himself into heaven.

Amen.

What does this mean?—Answer.

That I should be certain that these petitions are acceptable to our Father in heaven and heard; for He Himself has commanded us so to pray, and has promised that He will hear us. Amen, Amen; that is, Yea, yea, it shall be so.

IV. The Sacrament of Holy Baptism

As the head of the family should teach it in a simple way to his household.

First.

What is Baptism?—Answer.

Baptism is not simple water only, but it is the water comprehended in God's command and connected with God's Word.

Which is that word of God?—Answer.

Christ, our Lord, says in the last chapter of Matthew: *Go ye into all the world and teach all nations, baptizing them in the name of the Father, and of the Son, and of the Holy Ghost.*

Secondly.

What does Baptism give or profit?—Answer.

It works forgiveness of sins, delivers from death and the devil, and gives eternal salvation to all who believe this, as the words and promises of God declare.

Which are such words and promises of God? Answer.

Christ, our Lord, says in the last chapter of Mark: *He that believeth and is baptized shall be saved; but he that believeth not shall be damned.*

Thirdly.

How can water do such great things?—Answer.

It is not the water indeed that does them, but the word of God which is in and with the water, and faith, which trusts such word of God in the water. For without the word of God the water is simple water and no baptism. But with the word of God it is a baptism, that is, a gracious water of life and a washing of regeneration in the Holy Ghost, as St. Paul says, Titus, chapter three: *By the washing of regeneration and renewing of the Holy Ghost, which He shed on us abundantly through Jesus Christ, our Savior, that, being justified by*

His grace, we should be made heirs according to the hope of eternal life. This is a faithful saying.

Fourthly.

What does such baptizing with water signify?—Answer.

It signifies that the old Adam in us should, by daily contrition and repentance, be drowned and die with all sins and evil lusts, and, again, a new man daily come forth and arise; who shall live before God in righteousness and purity forever.

Where is this written?—Answer.

St. Paul says Romans, chapter 6: *We are buried with Christ by Baptism into death, that, like as He was raised up from the dead by the glory of the Father, even so we also should walk in newness of life.*

V. CONFESSION

How Christians should be taught to confess.

[What is Confession?—Answer.]

Confession embraces two parts: the one is, that we confess our sins; the other, that we receive absolution, or forgiveness, from the confessor, as from God Himself, and in no wise doubt, but firmly believe, that our sins are thereby forgiven before God in heaven.

What sins should we confess? — [Answer.]

Before God we should plead guilty of all sins, even of those which we do not know, as we do in the Lord's Prayer. But before the confessor we should confess those sins alone which we know and feel in our hearts.

Which are these? — [Answer.]

Here consider your station according to the Ten Commandments, whether you are a father, mother, son, daughter, master, mistress, a man-servant or maid-servant; whether you have been disobedient, unfaithful, slothful; whether you have grieved any one by words or deeds; whether you have stolen, neglected, or wasted aught, or done other injury.

Pray, Propose to Me a Brief Form of Confession.

Answer.

You should speak to the confessor thus: Reverend and dear sir, I beseech you to hear my confession, and to pronounce forgiveness to me for God's sake.

Proceed!

I, a poor sinner, confess myself before God guilty of all sins; especially I confess before you that I am a man-servant, a maidservant, etc. But, alas, I serve my master unfaithfully; for in this and in that I have not done what they commanded me; I have provoked them, and caused them to curse, have been negligent [in many things] and permitted damage to be done; have also been immodest in words and deeds, have quarreled with my equals, have grumbled and sworn at my mistress, etc. For all this I am sorry, and pray for grace; I want to do better.

A master or mistress may say thus:

In particular I confess before you that I have not faithfully trained my children, domestics, and wife [family] for God's glory. I have cursed, set a bad example by rude words and deeds, have done my neighbor harm and spoken evil of him, have overcharged and given false ware and short measure.

And whatever else he has done against God's command and his station, etc.

But if any one does not find himself burdened with such or greater sins, he should not trouble himself or search for or invent other sins, and thereby make confession a torture, but mention one or two that he knows. Thus: In particular I confess that I once cursed; again, I once used improper words, I have once neglected this or that, etc. Let this suffice.

But if you know of none at all (which, however is scarcely possible), then mention none in particular, but receive the forgiveness upon your general confession which you make before God to the confessor.

Then shall the confessor say:

God be merciful to thee and strengthen thy faith! Amen.

Furthermore:

Dost thou believe that my forgiveness is God's forgiveness?

Answer.

Yes, dear sir.

Then let him say:

As thou believest, so be it done unto thee. And by the command of our Lord Jesus Christ I forgive thee thy sins, in the name of the Father and of the Son and of the Holy Ghost. Amen. Depart in peace.

But those who have great burdens upon their consciences, or are distressed and tempted, the confessor will know how to comfort and to encourage to faith with more passages of Scripture. This is to be merely a general form of confession for the unlearned.

VI. THE SACRAMENT OF THE ALTAR

As the head of the family should teach it in a simple way to his household.

What is the Sacrament of the Altar?—Answer.

It is the true body and blood of our Lord Jesus Christ, under the bread and wine, for us Christians to eat and to drink, instituted by Christ Himself.

Where is this written?—Answer.

The holy Evangelists, Matthew, Mark, Luke, and St. Paul, write thus:

Our Lord Jesus Christ, the same night in which He was betrayed, took bread: and when He had given thanks, He brake it, and gave it to His disciples, and said, Take, eat; this is My body, which is given for you. This do in remembrance of Me.

After the same manner also He took the cup, when He had supped, gave thanks, and gave it to them, saying, Take, drink ye all of it. This cup is the new testament in My blood, which is shed for you for the remission of sins. This do ye, as oft as ye drink it, in remembrance of Me.

What is the benefit of such eating and drinking?—Answer.

That is shown us in these words: *Given, and shed for you, for the remission of sins*; namely, that in the Sacrament forgiveness of sins, life, and salvation are given us through these words. For where there is forgiveness of sins, there is also life and salvation.

How can bodily eating and drinking do such great things?—Answer.

It is not the eating and drinking, indeed, that does them, but the words which stand here, namely: *Given, and shed for you, for the remission of sins.* Which words are, beside the bodily eating and drinking, as the chief thing in the Sacrament; and he that believes these words has what they say and express, namely, the forgiveness of sins.

Who, then, receives such Sacrament worthily?—Answer.

Fasting and bodily preparation is, indeed, a fine outward training; but he is truly worthy and well prepared who has faith in these words: *Given, and shed for you, for the remission of sins.*

But he that does not believe these words, or doubts, is unworthy and unfit; for the words For you require altogether believing hearts.

APPENDIX I.

HOW THE HEAD OF THE FAMILY

Should Teach His Household to Bless Themselves in the Morning and in the Evening.

Morning Prayer.

In the morning, when you rise, you shall bless yourself with the holy cross and say:

In the name of God the Father, Son, and Holy Ghost. Amen.

Then, kneeling or standing, repeat the Creed and the Lord's Prayer. If you choose, you may, in addition, say this little prayer:

I thank Thee, my Heavenly Father, through Jesus Christ, Thy dear Son, that Thou hast kept me this night from all harm and danger; and I pray Thee to keep me this day also from sin and all evil, that all my doings and life may please Thee. For into Thy hands I commend myself, my body and soul, and all things. Let Thy holy angel be with me, that the Wicked Foe may have no power over me. Amen.

Then go to your work with joy, singing a hymn, as the Ten Commandments, or what your devotion may suggest.

Evening Prayer.

In the evening, when you go to bed, you shall bless yourself with the holy cross and say:

In the name of God the Father, Son, and Holy Ghost. Amen.

Then, kneeling or standing, repeat the Creed and the Lord's Prayer. If you choose, you may, in addition, say this little prayer:

I thank Thee, my Heavenly Father, through Jesus Christ, Thy dear Son, that Thou hast graciously kept me this day, and I pray Thee to forgive me all my sins, where I have done wrong, and graciously keep me this night. For into Thy hands I commend myself, my body and soul, and all things. Let Thy holy angel be with me, that the Wicked Foe may have no power over me. Amen.

Then go to sleep promptly and cheerfully.

HOW THE HEAD OF THE FAMILY

Should Teach His Household to Ask a Blessing and Return Thanks.

[Asking a Blessing.]

The children and servants shall go to the table with folded hands and reverently, and say:

The eyes of all wait upon Thee, O Lord; and Thou givest them their meat in due season; Thou openest Thine hand, and satisfiest the desire of every living thing.

Note.

To satisfy the desire means that all animals receive so much to eat that they are on this account joyful and of good cheer; for care and avarice hinder such satisfaction.

Then the Lord's Prayer, and the prayer here following:

Lord God, Heavenly Father, bless us and these Thy gifts, which we take from Thy bountiful goodness, through Jesus Christ, our Lord. Amen.

Returning Thanks.

Likewise also after the meal they shall reverently and with folded hands say:

O give thanks unto the Lord, for He is good; for His mercy endureth forever. He giveth food to all flesh; He giveth to the beast his food, and to the young ravens which cry. He delighteth not in the strength of the horse; He taketh not pleasure in the legs of a man. The Lord taketh pleasure in them that fear Him, in those that hope in His mercy.

Then the Lord's Prayer and the prayer here following:

We thank Thee, Lord God, Father, through Jesus Christ, our Lord, for all Thy benefits, who livest and reignest forever and ever. Amen.

TABLE OF DUTIES

Certain of Certain Passages of Scripture for Various Holy Orders and Stations, Whereby These are to Admonished, as by a Special Lesson, Regarding Their Office and Service.

For Bishops, Pastors, and Preachers.

A bishop must be blameless, the husband of one wife, vigilant, sober, of good behavior, given to hospitality, apt to teach; not given to wine, no striker, not greedy of filthy lucre; but patient, not a brawler, not covetous; one that ruleth well his own house, having his children in subjection with all gravity; not a novice; holding fast the faithful Word as he hath been taught, that he may be able by sound doctrine both to exhort and to convince the gainsayers. 1 Tim. 3:2 ff ; Titus 1:6.

What the Hearers Owe to Their Pastors.

Even so hath the Lord ordained that they which preach the Gospel should live of the Gospel. 1 Cor. 9:14. Let him that is taught in the Word communicate unto him that teacheth in all good things. Gal. 6:6. Let the elders that rule well be counted worthy of double honor, especially they who labor in the Word and doctrine. For the Scripture saith, Thou shalt not muzzle the ox that treadeth out the corn; and the laborer is worthy of his reward. 1 Tim. 5:17-18. Obey them that have the rule over you, and submit yourselves; for they watch for your souls as they that must give account, that they may do it with joy and not with grief; for that is unprofitable for you. Heb. 13:17.]

Concerning Civil Government.

Let every soul be subject unto the higher powers. For the power which exists anywhere is ordained of God. Whosoever resisteth the power resisteth the ordinance of God; and they that resist shall receive to themselves damnation. For he beareth not the sword in vain; for he is the minister of God, a revenger to execute wrath upon him that doeth evil. Rom. 13:1-4.

What Subjects Owe to the Magistrates.

Render unto Caesar the things which are Caesar's. Matt. 22:21. Let every soul be subject unto the higher powers, etc. Wherefore ye must needs be subject, not only for wrath, but also for conscience' sake. For, for this cause pay ye tribute also; for they are God's ministers, attending continually upon this very thing. Render therefore to all their dues: tribute to whom tribute is due; custom, to whom custom; fear, to whom fear; honor, to whom honor. Rom. 13:1,5ff. I exhort, therefore, that, first of all, supplications, prayers, intercessions, and giving of thanks be made for all men; for kings and for all that are in authority, that we may lead a quiet and peaceable life in all godliness and honesty. 1 Tim. 2:1f Put them in mind to be subject to principalities and powers, etc. Titus 3:1. Submit yourselves to every ordinance of man for the Lord's sake, whether it be to the king as supreme, or unto governors as unto them that are sent by him, etc. 1 Pet. 2:13f]

For Husbands.

Ye husbands, dwell with your wives according to knowledge, giving honor unto the wife, as unto the weaker vessel, and as being heirs together of the grace of life, that your prayers be not hindered. 1

Pet. 3:7. And be not bitter against them. Col. 3:9.

For Wives.

Wives, submit yourselves unto your own husbands, as unto the Lord, even as Sarah obeyed Abraham, calling him lord; whose daughters ye are, as long as ye do well, and are not afraid with any amazement. 1 Pet. 3:6; Eph. 5:22.

For Parents.

Ye fathers, provoke not your children to wrath, but bring them up in the nurture and admonition of the Lord. Eph. 6:4.

For Children.

Children, obey your parents in the Lord; for this is right. Honor thy father and mother; which is the first commandment with promise: that it may be well with thee, and thou mayest live long on the earth. Eph. 6:1-3.

For Male and Female Servants, Hired Men, and Laborers.

Servants, be obedient to them that are your masters according to the flesh, with fear and trembling, in singleness of your heart, as unto Christ; not with eye-service, as men-pleasers, but as the servants of Christ, doing the will of God from the heart; with good will doing service as to the Lord, and not to men; knowing that whatsoever good thing any man doeth, the same shall he receive of the Lord, whether he be bond or free. Eph. 6:5ff; Col. 3:22.

For Masters and Mistresses.

Ye masters, do the same things unto them, forbearing threatening, knowing that your Master also is in heaven; neither is there respect of persons with Him. Eph. 6:9; Col. 4:1.

For Young Persons in General.

Likewise, ye younger, submit yourselves unto the elder. Yea, all of you be subject one to another, and be clothed with humility; for God resisteth the proud, and giveth grace to the humble. Humble yourselves, therefore, under the mighty hand of God that He may exalt you in due time. 1 Pet. 5:5-6.

For Widows.

She that is a widow indeed, and desolate, trusteth in God, and continueth in supplications and prayers night and day. But she that liveth in pleasure is dead while she liveth. 1 Tim. 5:5-6.

For All in Common.

Thou shalt love thy neighbor as thyself. Herein are comprehended all the commandments. Rom. 13:8ff And persevere in prayer for all men. 1 Tim. 2:1-2.

> Let each his lesson learn with care,
> And all the household well shall fare.

Christian Questions with Their Answers

Prepared by Dr. Martin Luther for those who intend to go to the Sacrament

[The "Christian Questions with Their Answers," designating Luther as the author, first appeared in an edition of the Small Catechism in 1551, five years after Luther's death].

After confession and instruction in the Ten Commandments, the Creed, the Lord's Prayer, and the Sacraments of Baptism and the Lord's Supper, the pastor may ask, or Christians may ask themselves these questions:

1. Do you believe that you are a sinner?

Yes, I believe it. I am a sinner.

2. How do you know this?

From the Ten Commandments, which I have not kept.

3. Are you sorry for your sins?

Yes, I am sorry that I have sinned against God.

4. What have you deserved from God because of your sins?

His wrath and displeasure, temporal death, and eternal damnation. See Romans 6:21,23.

5. Do you hope to be saved?

Yes, that is my hope.

6. In whom then do you trust?

In my dear Lord Jesus Christ.

7. Who is Christ?

The Son of God, true God and man.

8. How many Gods are there?

Only one, but there are three persons: Father, Son, and Holy Spirit.

9. What has Christ done for you that you trust in Him?

He died for me and shed His blood for me on the cross for the forgiveness of sins.

10. Did the Father also die for you?

He did not. The Father is God only, as is the Holy Spirit; but the Son is both true God and true man. He died for me and shed his blood for me.

11. How do you know this?

From the holy Gospel, from the words instituting the Sacrament, and by His body and blood given me as a pledge in the Sacrament.

12. What are the Words of Institution?

Our Lord Jesus Christ, on the night when He was betrayed, took bread and when He had given thanks, He broke it and gave it to the disciples and said: "Take eat; this is My body, which is given for you. This do in remembrance of Me." In the same way also He took the cup after supper, and when He had given thanks, He gave it to them, saying: "Drink of it, all of you; this cup is the new testament in My blood, which is shed for you for the forgiveness of sins. This do, as often as you drink it, in remembrance of Me."

> *13. Do you believe, then, that the true body and blood*
> *of Christ are in the Sacrament?*

Yes, I believe it.

> *14. What convinces you to believe this?*

The word of Christ: Take, eat, this is My body; drink of it, all of you, this is My blood.

> *15. What should we do when we eat His body and drink His blood, and*
> *in this way receive His pledge?*

We should remember and proclaim His death and the shedding of His blood, as He taught us: This do, as often as you drink it, in remembrance of Me.

> *16. Why should we remember and proclaim His death?*

First, so that we may learn to believe that no creature could make satisfaction for our sins. Only Christ, true God and man, could do that. Second, so we may learn to be horrified by our sins, and to regard them as very serious. Third, so we may find joy and comfort in Christ alone, and through faith in Him be saved.

> *17. What motivated Christ to die and make full payment for your sins?*

His great love for His Father and for me and other sinners, as it is written in John 14; Romans 5; Galatians 2 and Ephesians 5.

> *18. Finally, why do you wish to go to the Sacrament?*

That I may learn to believe that Christ, out of great love, died for my sin, and also learn from Him to love God and my neighbor.

> *19. What should admonish and encourage a Christian to*
> *receive the Sacrament frequently?*

First, both the command and the promise of Christ the Lord. Second, his own pressing need, because of which the command, encouragement, and promise are given.

*20. But what should you do if you are not aware of this need
and have no hunger and thirst for the Sacrament?*

To such a person no better advice can be given than this: first, he should touch his body to see if he still has flesh and blood. Then he should believe what the Scriptures say of it in Galatians 5 and Romans 7. Second, he should look around to see whether he is still in the world, and remember that there will be no lack of sin and trouble, as the Scriptures say in John 15-16 and in 1 John 2 and 5. Third, he will certainly have the devil also around him, who with his lying and murdering day and night will let him have no peace, within or without, as the Scriptures picture him in John 8 and 16; 1 Peter 5; Ephesians 6; and 2 Timothy 2.

Note:

These questions and answers are no child's play, but are drawn up with great earnestness of purpose by the venerable and devout Dr. Luther for both young and old. Let each one pay attention and consider it a serious matter; for St. Paul writes to the Galatians in chapter six: "Do not be deceived: God cannot be mocked."

THE END

Made in the USA
Monee, IL
15 April 2021